Let's Draw!

Design

Leon Baxter

Collins
in association with
Belitha Press

Let's draw together . . .

In the first six *Let's Draw!* books you discovered the basic principles of line, colour, movement, shape and proportion. If you have tried all those ideas, you should now be feeling more confident about making pictures.

   In these new books I am encouraging you to be observant and inventive so that you will enjoy your drawing even more. You can learn how to compose and construct your pictures, how to create space and movement, and even how to have three-dimensional fun with paper itself.

   Don't use a ruler. Draw all straight lines freehand. This is a good exercise for getting your eyes and hands to work together. Try out some of these ideas. Use your imagination and see your paper come to life.

Things you will need:

coloured pencils	paint	glue
crayons	sticky coloured paper	brushes
pastels	lots of drawing paper (white and coloured)	scissors
felt-tip pens		

Have a good time!

Leon Baxter

First published 1989 by William Collins Sons and Co Ltd
in association with Belitha Press Limited,
31 Newington Green, London N16 9PU
Text and illustrations in this format copyright © Belitha Press 1989
Text and illustrations copyright © Leon Baxter 1989
Art Director: Treld Bicknell   Editor: Carol Watson
ISBN 0 00 197791 1
Typesetting by Chambers Wallace, London
Printed in Italy

What is design?

To **design** is to plan or invent something so that it does its job properly. There is design in nature. All natural things have to obey rules in order to exist. These rules of design make the world beautiful and interesting.

Colour the picture.

Rainfall is part of a well-designed plan in nature. The sun shining over the sea makes water rise and form clouds. The clouds then move over the land where the water falls from the clouds as rain. Clouds come in all shapes and sizes.

Clouds and rain are fun to draw.

What cloud shapes do you like? Draw them here.

When raindrops fall, they are heavier at the bottom and so they form beautiful tear shapes.

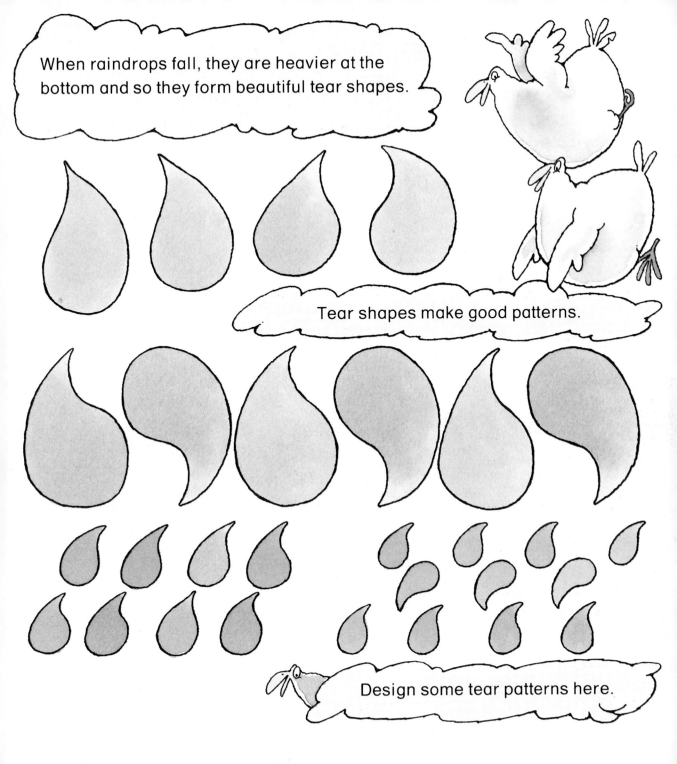

Tear shapes make good patterns.

Design some tear patterns here.

5

Once it has fallen as rain, water has to get back to the sea. Little streams come together to form rivers.

Water cannot flow uphill or through mountains, so it has to find its way around them.

Flowing water makes sweeping, curved shapes.

Draw a picture of clouds, rain, streams and rivers in this nice big space.

Plants live by rules, too.

In order to live, flowers must grow roots downwards to drink and leaves and petals outwards and upwards to reach the sun. All flowers obey these rules, but they come in lots of different shapes, colour and sizes.

rose

tulip

I have drawn two flowers.

A tree must grow roots firmly down into the ground and branches out and up, so that the sun can shine on its leaves. Leaves are also designed to obey the rules, but they also grow in different shapes and sizes – some are broad and flat and some are thin and pointed.

Oak

Yew

I have drawn two sorts of leaves.

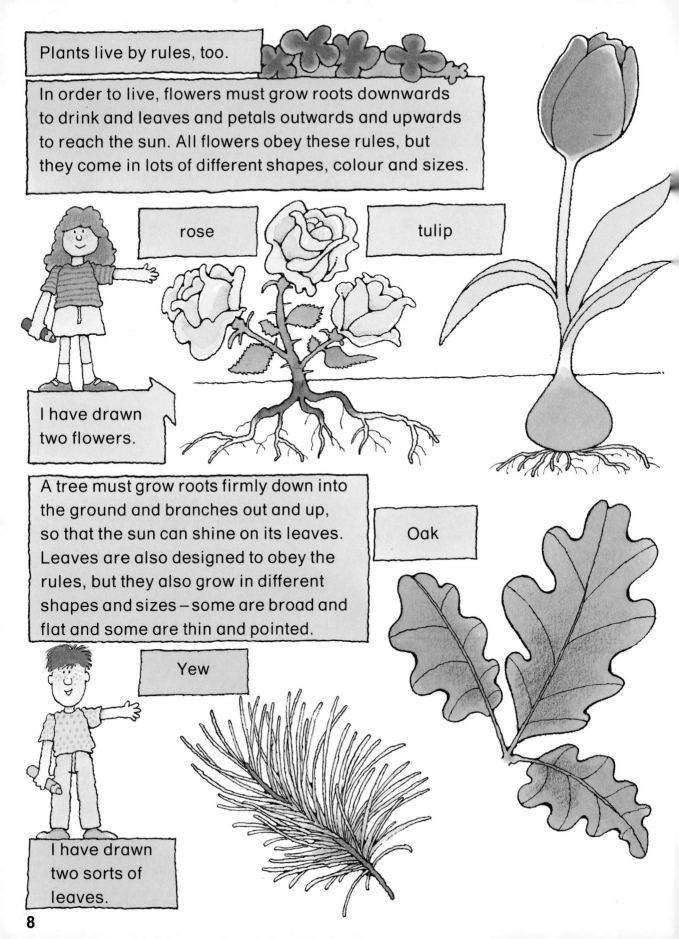

Draw one of your favourite flowers –
then design a new one.

Which leaves do you like? Draw them here.

Animals come in many shapes and sizes. Their bodies are designed to help them survive wherever they live.

A gazelle has strong legs so that it can run away from a lion.

Draw a gazelle escaping from a lion.

An elephant is very big so that even a lion will not harm it.
It needs a long trunk to reach up high to eat and down low to drink.

Can you draw an elephant eating or drinking?

Animals are all sorts of colours.
Colour has a job to do.

Zebras are hunted by other animals.
Their pattern of black and white stripes
helps them to hide in the long grass.

Draw a zebra hiding.

Butterflies don't hide but their bright colours warn others: 'Keep
away, I'm not good to eat'.

Design some brightly-coloured butterflies.

When people design things they also have to follow rules. Things have to be the right size and shape.

Think how difficult it would be to have a hot drink if somebody had not designed a cup or mug to put it in.

A cup or a mug has to be the right size to hold the drink. The base has to be broad enough to balance the weight of the drink, and it needs a handle to stop you from burning your fingers.

This engine is too small to pull these coaches.

Can you design a bigger engine?

A cup or mug must do its job, but can be designed in different ways.

This is my mug.

Can you design your own cup or mug?

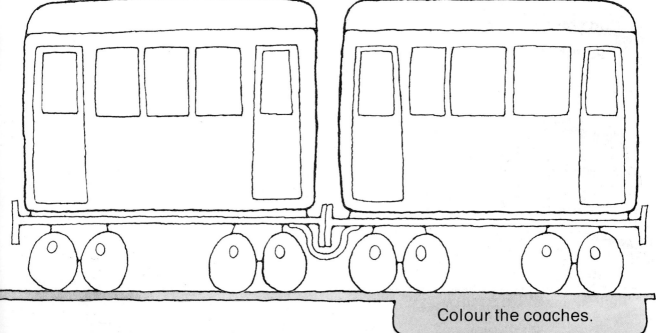

Colour the coaches.

People often use colour to do a special job. Red is a warning colour and green is a safety colour. These colours were used in the design of traffic lights.

Which chair was designed for which person to use?

Write your answers here.

Which traffic light shows red and which shows green?

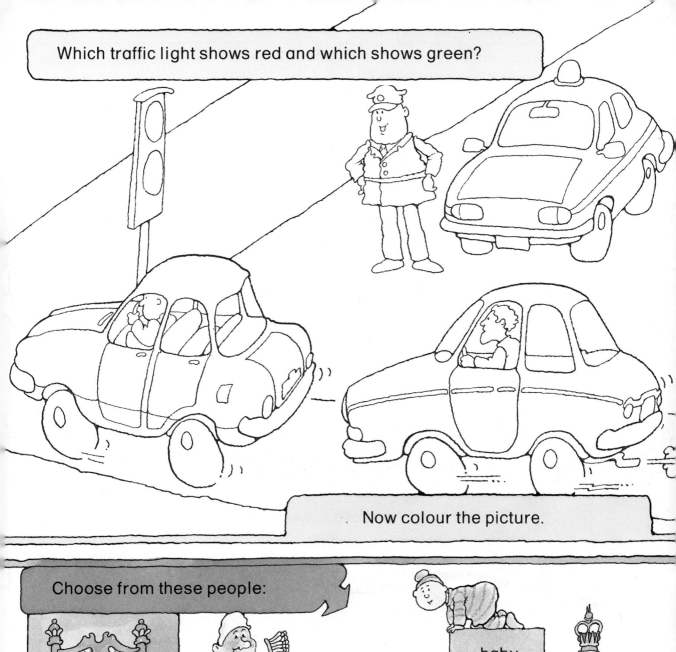

Now colour the picture.

Choose from these people:

baby

dentist

grandpa

queen

Colours

Things can be made to work better by changing their size, shape or colour. If you want to be designers, you'll need to think about size, shape and colour, too.

Let's take a closer look at colours.

This is a rainbow.

Colour this one.

The colours of the rainbow form a 'colour circle'.

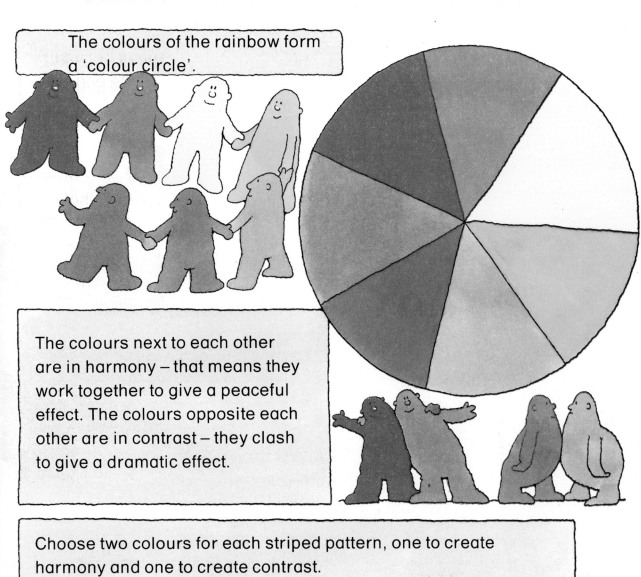

The colours next to each other are in harmony – that means they work together to give a peaceful effect. The colours opposite each other are in contrast – they clash to give a dramatic effect.

Choose two colours for each striped pattern, one to create harmony and one to create contrast.

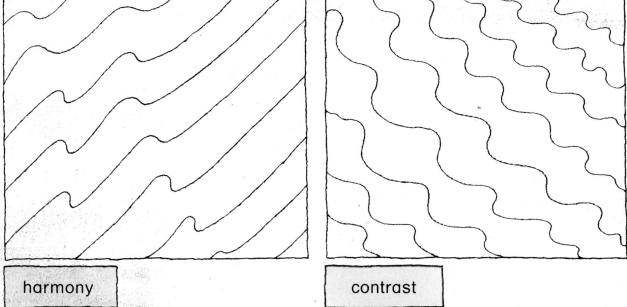

harmony

contrast

Shapes

Shapes too can be in harmony and contrast.

harmony

These curved lines could be rolling hills or waves on a lake.

Design a pattern of shapes and colours in harmony.

Design a pattern of shapes and colours in contrast.

contrast

The sharp lines could be jagged rocks or the teeth of a monster.

Draw a picture of two dragons fighting. Use both curved shapes and jagged shapes. You may want to use a large piece of paper.

Size

Make the missing house the same size to finish this row of houses in *harmony*.

Complete this row of houses in *contrast* by making the missing house smaller.

Here are some houses. Finish them by designing their windows and doors in lots of different sizes.

Now colour them.

Let's design a street scene.

Can you finish the houses, draw some cars and dress the people?
Remember to use harmony and contrast in shapes, sizes and colours.

This car has been designed to go fast.

Draw a truck that is designed to carry a heavy load.

These clothes were designed for a hot sunny day.

Draw someone wearing clothes designed for a wet and windy day.